QUEEN KONG

Other Books by Amanda J. Bradley

Hints and Allegations (NYQ Books, 2009)
Oz at Night (NYQ Books, 2011)

Queen Kong

Amanda J. Bradley

NYQ Books™

The New York Quarterly Foundation, Inc.
New York, New York

NYQ Books™ is an imprint of The New York Quarterly Foundation, Inc.

The New York Quarterly Foundation, Inc.
P. O. Box 2015
Old Chelsea Station
New York, NY 10113

www.nyq.org

First Edition

Set in New Baskerville

Layout by Raymond P. Hammond

Cover Art by Mikayla Lewis

Library of Congress Control Number: 2017930503

ISBN: 978-1-63045-038-0

Queen Kong

Acknowledgements

Grateful acknowledgement is made to the editors of the following anthology and journals in which these poems first appeared: "City to Country," "Polluted Sunsets," "A Straight Shot," and "Ricketts Glen" in *Down the Dog Hole: 11 Poets on Northeast Pennsylvania,* "Changing Hands" in *Broad! Magazine,* "Mean" and "Rite of Rebellion" in *Skidrow Penthouse,* "I Read People by What They Read" in *Paterson Literary Review,* "Swallowed Whole" in *THEthe Poetry Blog,* and "Escapist," "Why Do English Majors Have to Analyze Everything to Death?" and "Plants on the Moon" in *Ragazine.*

Contents

Belonging

Outpourings

Revolting

For the family I grew up with:
my mother, Nicki Bradley; my father, Mike Bradley; and my brother, Eric Bradley.
I am eternally grateful to you for rescuing me from so many brinks
with your unconditional love.

Belonging

I. Eight

I am beginning to realize how much I exist. I am really a person,
and these are my thoughts, my hands, my eyes in the mirror.
I care about what I am wearing. I listen to Blondie and the soundtrack
to *Grease*. In the summertime, we leave home in the morning
and only return for food. We climb trees and shake the limbs hard
to litter the ground with buckeyes for Jess's mom to paint tiny,
magical images on them. We tie jump ropes to bike seats, don roller skates,
and sling each other around corners. Dogs follow us to the kickball field
and watch our playground politics as we pick teams. We imitate each others'
dives and do cannonballs into the pool at the Dolphin Club to splash
the adults on their lawn chairs. On rainy days, we play with Barbie dolls
and Matchbox cars, try to beat each others' scores at *Space Invaders*.
We chew Bazooka bubblegum, stuff our cheeks with it, and spit
on the softball field because that's how the real players do with tobacco.
We play Joan Jett on the jukebox at the ice cream parlor after games.
We sleep over at each others' houses and ask the Ouija board spooky
questions, stick celery up the nose of the first to sleep. We grope
each other in the dark and trace fingers lightly down each other's backs.
We collect fuzzy caterpillars at recess and sneak them into our pencil boxes.
I am an avid reader, excel at Double Dutch jump rope and hand jive routines.
I try so hard. I am quiet but a leader nonetheless. I can be cruel because
it is important to me to be strong. I am cute and make some people nervous.

We load up the car with travel games and snacks and trek to Saint Louis
where we lurch to the top of the arch, gateway to the west, in capsule
elevators that tilt and nod their way up. Next we head for Houston
to see my godparents and their kids. It is humid, and I am appalled
by the size of the bugs. I develop a kid crush on their oldest son.
On the way back up, we stop in New Orleans. As we drive into the city
at noon, a man comes hurtling out of a corner bar, staggering backwards
and falling, his face bloody. Another man runs out after him, arm raised
to strike again. He changes his mind, hops on a bicycle, buzzes off.
I see a litter of unattended kittens as we eat beignets in the park
by the river where so many strutting pigeons make Mom nervous.
The city seems exotic and edgy; its idiosyncrasy appeals to me.

At Halloween, the garage becomes haunted. Spaghetti and peeled grapes
become guts and eyeballs in a bowl. Ann dresses like a zombie to jump out
and scare the little ones, and Jess becomes a gypsy fortune teller
in hooped earrings and a purple scarf before her makeshift crystal ball.
We bob for apples and eat our trick-or-treating candy in the driveway.

Christmas is the best time of the year. It's Mom's favorite holiday,
and she makes it feel fairy tale, decorates the house with white lights
and silver tinsel. She teases us about what Santa may bring. We carefully
select gifts we buy with our allowance at the Winter Festival at school.
We sing carols in the neighborhood and at the city's children's hospital.
"Gloria in excelsis Deo" and "Joy to the World" and candles light up
reverent church services. Grandma comes to visit and rolls out dough,
makes green and red icing to decorate the Christmas cookies.
We sled at a nearby park, and our dog Jack runs alongside, barking.

We are middle class in the mid-sized town of Anderson, Indiana,
Middle America. I cannot imagine a better way to be young.
When I learn we are moving to Georgia, it sounds like an adventure.
It also feels terrifying, daunting. Anderson is already my third city,
but Cincinnati and Pittsburgh seem distant memories. I consider
the friends I left behind and lost in those moves. The movers
have boxed my room. I climb to the top shelf of the closet
in my bedroom and wonder at how strange to be leaving, how strange
my friends should go on without me in the thick of it with them,
how strange to see my pink and green and yellow room dotted in boxes,
to be sitting atop empty shelves, surveying and wondering what comes next.

II. Twelve

It is lush and warm in Marietta, Georgia, with azaleas and kudzu lining
the Chattanooga River. I learn the malls because I love to shop. I love pink.
I love ballet and tap. May I wear makeup yet? My parents are happier here,
especially my mom. I swim on a team and play tennis, and my brother and I
skateboard up and down the hills around our neighborhood. We swing
from vines over the creek behind our house and find a grove to be our fort.
We draw up Rules of the Secret Club. I start to babysit and get spooked watching
Fantasy Island once I've put the kids to bed. I stalk around the house with
a wooden duck over my head to hit the intruders, but it's just the parents
arriving home. I stare at a hot dog in water in a pot, trying to figure out how
to cook dinner, am amazed to be entrusted with other people's children.

We go to Myrtle Beach and Hilton Head, where we swim in the salt water,
play with buckets in the sand, and admire the heavy branches and roots
of ancient live oak trees. One spring, when the cherry blossoms bloom,
we fly to Washington DC. My dad embarrasses us by repeatedly saying "far out,"
an outdated phrase, so we all start saying it at the Smithsonian and monuments.
My family is goofy and fun, close knit. Moving makes us need each other more.

The schools are terrible, and my parents send us to a private Christian school.
Soon, I am writing in my little red journal about how much I love Jesus
and also Sam who sits next to me. The teachers tell us rock and roll is evil,
so I tear up my cassettes of Michael Jackson, Queen, Prince, and Adam Ant.
Hidden in the backseat of the bus, I kiss bad boy Sam, sent here to clean up
his act. I become more popular than I have ever been before in this tiny school.
I am elected student body president. Students and teachers form a very long
line down the hallway for me to sign their yearbooks, and I think this cannot be
normal. I get my period. The cramps are so painful. This cannot be normal.
I do and do not want to be both normal and special. I ask my teacher
"Is it a sin to masturbate?" She blanches and spits. "Why doesn't God
have a wife?" I want to know. When the administrators learn we are moving
to Texas, they ask me to speak at the final school assembly. I read a poem
I wrote with doves and angel wings. Everyone is saying "Go with God" and
"Peace in Christ" through tears. We throw a going away party. On the scavenger
hunt around our neighborhood, Sam gets in a fight with a bully. I admire him
for it. I do not remember the boxes at that house, just Sam's bloody shirt
and his eyes that showed he genuinely cared that I was leaving.

III. Fourteen

Long, blonde curls fly behind as I careen through Plano, Texas
neighborhoods, past red brick ranch houses on my blue ten speed,
limbs strong and lithe from years of ballet. I begin to taste freedom.
My poems begin to flutter into existence. I write them in my rainbow-
hearted bedroom, newly discovered Plath my inspiration. I sprawl
across my twin bed, swallowing books, soon to be released from braces.

We pack too much luggage for Paris and London. We have to take
two taxis to the hotel. I have a suitcase of shoes. We see the *Mona Lisa*
and Monet's *Water Lilies*. I am transformed by Rembrandt, by moving
among people I can barely understand. We eat escargot in the hotel bar.
I am fascinated by Montmartre, the stories of the artists, the histories
of romance. My mother tells me not to swing my hips. I see the men watching.
I wonder what champagne is like, wine, gin and tonic. My brother
and I climb the lions in Trafalgar Square. I admire the poets buried
at Westminster. We trudge to the top of St. Paul's Cathedral.
I cry at a production of *Cats,* knowing nothing of T.S. Eliot.

At school, I am a nerd and don't mind much except the guys are less
likely to notice me this way. Between dolls and dalliance, I begin
to realize my body can be a weapon, can be violated, can be impregnated,
can make me strong or weak. I start high school. My English teacher says
I write well. She says Justin writes well, too. We begin to talk on the phone.
I lie on my parents' bed and wind the phone cord though my fingers.
I catch myself in the mirror. I can see he makes me feel happy. I feel pretty
and smart all at once. This is important to me. "May I have this dance?"
he wants to know. We dance to Bryan Adams' "Heaven." He asks for more,
but there are rebellious boys who have moved a lot like me, who will take me
to OMD concerts and teach me about clove cigarettes. I say no. Instead, I go out
with the one who will soon have a mohawk. When I am told we are moving,
I grab matches from the kitchen and ride far to a distant park. I strike them
one by one, attempting to put them out on my wet, pink tongue, terrifying
myself, waiting for cars to pass, till I am alone, before trying again. At last,
I succeed. I settle fire in my mouth. I swing upside down from a bar on the
playground. I am a fire-eating acrobat with no fear. I can do, I can be anything.

IV. Fifteen

We are west now, in Omaha, Nebraska, in the land of cattle, buffalo,
and jack-a-lope jokes. Our house soars and juts. Our homes are getting bigger.
I have stretched a hamstring too far and down go dreams of dancing.
I take up tennis. I have decided my body will be a weapon. I wear sweater
dresses and lace hose, low heels and lipstick to debate seniors from other schools.
I will disarm them. One calls me sexy before the judges arrive. It is very
important to win. I do. I do. I do. Yes, Matt. Yes, Brent. Yes, Bill.
I am filling with desire. It rages through me in the basement, in the backs
of cars parked near the tracks, at parties I've lied to my parents to attend.
Stop. Stop. Stop. Don't make me pregnant or I will kick you in the balls
with these strong legs. My Texan friends and I write letters. Justin sends
a cassette tape on which he talks to me. It feels very intimate, as I listen
in my parents' Camry parked in the driveway, for privacy. The Texans
are becoming best friends without me. They are falling in love with each other.
My heart is vaguely breaking. Elaine encloses a picture from Homecoming.
She said yes to Justin. He towers over her in his suit. He is tall now.

On our way to Cancun, my parents announce another move.
I nearly fall from the narrow steps of a Mayan pyramid in Chichen Itza.
There are chickens outside hovels as we pass on the bus. I begin
to sense how unjust this world is. I want to be a serious person.
My dad leaves the bullfight. I follow him, tears hidden behind giant
sunglasses. It's so unfair. Mariachis are approaching our table,
this abundant spread of camarones tapatios, pineapple fajitas.
Buenos noches as tears fill my eyes again. I am failing at becoming
a bourgeois person. I am being trained, and I am failing.

I become more devious and reckless, buy cigarettes from a machine
in a restaurant lobby I've scoped out near the movie theaters, shimmy down
a sheet tied to the bed and hung out the window to meet one guy, make out
with another, Andrea's boyfriend, at a dance. Janey's sister answers the door
in a bra. I hope I don't have to take off my shirt to be here. I really want
to be here. Some seniors teach me Quarters. I down a lot of beer. I look up at the
whirring fan. This is ecstasy. "Gotta buzz?" someone asks. I love that word. I love
this feeling. The night before the truck is loaded, I let some friends into our
boxed up house, press the code into the alarm system. We listen
to *Licensed to Ill* on a boom box in the dark to avoid suspicion from the
neighborhood security cops. We smoke cigarettes. We feel time moving forward.

V. Sixteen

The flora and fauna are foreign again. There are pine tree forests with short
underbrush. Here magnolia dot vast, manicured lawns. Our house is a
Spanish mansion on a prominent street in El Dorado, Arkansas, an oil town.
I adore its winding staircase, its white columns, its brown and gray tiles.
The neighbor lady brings over a basket with wine and chicken salad and
local delicacies. Her southern drawl purrs through the house. My brother's
face beams when she invites us to use their pool. She will eventually
intimate it's inappropriate for us to mow the lawn ourselves. She has the black
help do it. I cannot make sense of how people relate here. They are sweet
as peaches but crack at each other behind backs. They are polite and
disingenuous and funny. I have trouble being these things. Angela is in
my French class. She is different, and I fall in love with her. She has long,
blonde, curly hair like me, but high cheekbones and sleek arms. Her French
accent is perfect, and she plays piano beautifully. She wears funky vintage
clothes from Salvation Army—men's dress pants cinched at the waist
with a thick leather belt, fedoras, lace blouses. She is movie star beautiful.
She is filled with disdain for El Do. I can tell she will get out. We play tennis
while smoking cigarettes at the country club. We listen to *Rubber Soul*
as we practice our lines for the school play. We are silly. We are genuine.

The first time I see Pat, he cruises up in his copper '67 Mustang convertible.
There is something glorious about his confidence, the opulent show
he puts on. He is wearing Ray Bans and a ball cap. His lean, muscled arms
are accentuated by his sleeveless T-shirt. He is showing off for me.
An exhilarated smile settles on my face. I shield my eyes from the sun
with my hand so I can see him better. We are sitting on the dock of a pond,
feet dangling. "So this is the new girl?" he says. We sense how dramatic
we can be together, what a show we can put on for this shitty little town,
what a figure we will cut as we parade around, young and dazzling. I am surprised
when we really fall in love. He is the consummate southern gentleman.
He buys bottles of Dom Perignon for candlelit picnics on the shore of the pond
on his father's land. He sends dozens of pink roses with sweet notes
for no reason. They sit next to my bed in vases. His parents are divorced.
He calls his mother "The Witch." His father's a doctor, and they share
a bachelor pad with a pool table and mounted deer heads. He has freedom,
which I crave so much. I am jealous. He lives in the abandoned RC Cola
warehouse for awhile. Angela and Pat and I push each other around in
wheeled office chairs and write with marker on the walls, listening to
White Snake. Pat and I argue about the Japanese internment camps
we learned about in History. I say they were unfair. He chases me
through the halls of the school and punches the cement wall when I run
into the restroom. My dad says I am learning to think for myself.

I am a bona fide smoker now. I am drinking whenever I can, which is often.
The police pick me up in the McDonald's parking lot with one shoe, my purse
lost at some party. At the station, I drunkenly explain to the officer
that I get good grades, am competing with two guys for valedictorian.
I get caught in the middle of a drug ring bust and have to meet
with a parole officer. I am sneaking out of the house, and I am pulling out
my hair because Pat went to see Suzy in New Mexico. I am throwing
his class ring into the pond. We are so dramatic. We are so unstoppable.
Things are getting out of hand, my parents say, and my dad takes
a new job in Indiana. Boxes. Angela and Pat and I are sitting in the living
room, glum about the impending departure. My mom sings the Indiana University
fight song and dances around. She is going home to where she was raised.
I am simply losing people and places, losing people and places.

VI. Seventeen

Fort Wayne, Indiana is flat. Cornfields spread for miles, and hay bales sprinkle
fields across the horizon. It reminds me of another era when we raced
the rows of corn in Anderson as a child. That seems so long ago now. I feel
lonely thinking of it. Pat has moved here too, to attend a local college and
be near me. I am conflicted. I know I am too young to be so serious. I am
unsure I will ever marry. I come across to my new classmates as daring and
experienced, well-traveled and cosmopolitan. This seems funny to me,
but I embrace the image. I can drive now, and I tool around in a stick shift,
light blue Corolla listening to the Violent Femmes and Sonic Youth. I settle
into who I am. I am not concerned to be friends with a particular clique.
Justin has stopped sending letters. I miss him. I work at a local gourmet
coffee and ice cream shop in a posh, empty mall. I clean endlessly there
just to be doing something. I drive to seedier parts of town and become a regular
at Tom's Donuts, Coney Island Lunch. I decide I love dives because they feel
authentic to me. I am an impostor, but no one cares. I love the lack of interest
in me, my anonymity. A gay friend takes me to drag shows at The Other Side,
and I buy him male porn on Pearl Street. Pat has grown pale, feels out of sorts
when people do not converse at the grocery store. No one knows him here,
and he begins to wither. I am blossoming. He visits El Dorado then moves back.
I am often grounded for drinking and sneaking out of the house. I date a soccer
player from a Catholic high school and "lose my virginity." I still excel at English
and acting. I add Journalism, and we fight the school board over censorship.
I help start a chapter of Amnesty International. My clothes get funkier. I wear
mustard yellow tights and long scarves. My mom and I have coffee for me,
iced tea for her every day when I get home from school. We realize how close
we are now that I am older. Eric and I, too, have become fast friends.
We pal around, swap music, and keep each other's secrets. My dad still travels
for work, as he has all these years, but we talk to him on the phone, go fishing
weekends. The four of us have weathered much together and are closer
than most families. Friends wish their parents were so easy to talk to,
so loving and rational. Friends wish they were as close to their siblings.
I want to go to a good school for college. I have wanted this for a long time.
I have worked hard for it, studying Calculus and reading *Canterbury Tales* carefully
in my closet late at night once I've snuck back in. I have taken SAT Prep
courses, and I make the case in applications that I am adaptable, having
attended four high schools. I am savvy and can succeed anywhere.
Acceptances roll in. I decide to attend Northwestern University for Journalism.
I come home one day, and my mom says, "You have a letter from Justin."
I burst into tears, am surprised by the violence of my relief.

Senior year spring break a girlfriend and I go on a cruise to the Bahamas.
We bask in the sun in bright bikinis as the waiters dance to reggae
with piña coladas on their trays. I wear my prom dress to the Captain's Ball
and tango with an officer who has tattoos when he takes his shirt off.
We go clubbing in Nassau in open air bars with wild, pounding music.
During the last summer before I leave for college, I work at Steak 'n Shake
and Kmart. I am saving money. I do not have a curfew. I value the loosening
of strictures and smoke cigarettes, write poems into the wee hours
at the doughnut shop. I am looking forward to living near Chicago. I am
looking forward to quirky professors and tough classes. I am buying
sheets and towels and talking to Justin on the phone. I am looking forward.

PART TWO: COLLEGE

I. Freshman Year

The students here went to Country Day schools. Their fathers are CEOs
of companies we've heard of. They decide to go skiing in Vail Friday morning
and leave that afternoon. I did not know there was this much money
in the world. We hail from around the country, around the globe. Our accents
and skin colors and personalities are various. But it feels unreal to be surrounded
by so much intelligence and affluence, so many empowered, beautiful people.
Our dorm, Bobb McCulloch, is on north campus in the middle of the
fraternities. I room with Elaine, a friend from Texas. We are placed in "The Pit"
of this party dorm, where we are misfits. We deliberately exacerbate our
strangeness. We scare off rush counselors with Joy Division and odd clothes.
I cut holes in a green cloth hat with turquoise elephants on it and pull my hair
through the holes. We buy inflatable animals and name them all Bob.
We wear pink fur and brightly sequined dresses to Pumpkin Prom. Misplaced
artists among future lawyers and investment bankers, we revel in the bizarre.
Anjali and Alice next door do not know what to make of us at first, but eventually
we become good friends. Anjali cannot get drunk, so we buy Everclear to mix with
punch to remedy her sobriety. Everyone pukes but Anjali. We trudge to the library
and occupy study rooms for hours; they give us a modicum of privacy, and we can
converse without annoying other ambitious students. Classes are challenging
and intimidating. Professors are world-renowned in their fields. We see our
sociology professor on the news being interviewed about Kuwait. We make signs
"No Blood for Oil" and march to protest the Gulf War in the streets of Chicago.

There is no coddling. I love the freedom and responsibility. My journalism classes
are designed to weed out people who are not serious about reporting. I am writing
for the school newspaper and two magazines. I think I am serious, but Modern Theater
is my favorite course first quarter: Ibsen, O'Neill, Strindberg, Chekhov. Winter quarter
rolls around, and we are bundled up in parkas, unsure whom we may be passing
on campus. It is isolating to be so cold, but good for studying. We meet Jerome
from France. He and I are night owls together. We commandeer "The Gross Room,"
with its flat, yellow carpet and purple paint stains, its netless ping pong table
and lack of other furniture. We listen to Sinead O'Connor and The Police and talk
into the wee hours. We make a nightly trip to the rocks by Lake Michigan where we
can observe Chicago's skyline, the red glow hovering above it. Some nights we take
the El into the city to wander. We walk by frozen road signs coated in two inches of ice.
The Chicago lakeside winter is brutal and lingers into March. During finals week,
we all open our windows at the designated time for the cathartic primal scream.
We hurl our frustrated cries into the bitter air, and they echo between buildings.
Justin has gone to school in Dallas. He calls Elaine and me periodically and decides
to visit during his spring break. We are an awkward threesome on the El to Evanston
from O'Hare. We have danced. They have dated. We make it to campus in time

to see *Macbeth,* as planned. Justin and I smoke at intermission, and he tells me
it's called the Scottish play in theater circles because it will curse the production
to call it by name. It's odd to look up at him now, strange to see him again but taller,
with his deeper voice, so familiar now from a year of lengthy conversations.
He still makes me feel pretty and smart all at once. I realize I am a little in love
with him standing in the cold air surrounded by snowy sidewalk, lakefront at our backs.
My feelings are strong and deep and muddled. It will be a messy week, and I grin
a horrible, happy grin because he's really here, tying my past to my present.

Winter finally spills into spring. Pink and white buds sprout on trees. We are
wearing sandals and tank tops. I take a course in existentialist literature: Rilke, Mann,
Sartre, Camus. I am trying so hard, but the books are depressing. The determined
professor insists no, we are free to choose how we live, what we believe. The ideas
cavort in havoc in my mind but slowly, eventually start to coalesce. I am empowered
by my liberation from social expectation. I fill with questions and try to answer
them myself, from within. I review what and how I have been taught all my life.
I reject many things and keep many others. I am careening into free. I draw correlations
through history, across countries, across classes. There is so much to know.
It is Dillo Day. Everyone is inebriated in tie dye. Poi Dog Pondering is playing
on a stage. Glints from the sun lift off the nearby lake, sparkling like stars.
Giant orange and pink beach balls bounce over the upraised hands of the crowd.
Winter has been obliterated. We conquered it. We are all a little crazy and so alive.

II. Summer 1991

I am back in Fort Wayne with my family. Justin has moved to a studio apartment here.
I am a waitress at a restaurant on a country highway and a freelance reporter
for a local newspaper. Justin takes a job at Karma Records. He plays his guitar,
and we spend countless hours singing. He writes songs about us while I'm working
and plays them for me upon my return. He makes me feel relevant, my life significant
in a way I've never experienced before. He writes poems and reads novels. I dance
around the bed in jean shorts and cowboy boots, tank tops and vintage skirts.
It is a summer of rabid fucking. I have never had this much sex. I am enrapt. He plays
the first chords of Bad Company's "Feel Like Makin' Love" on his guitar as a tease
or closes the window. Physically, I feel glorious. Emotionally, I am consumed
by intensity. I am more sober than I've been in years. I am always weeping.
We drink coffee, and smoke cigarettes at Azar's Big Boy until two in the morning.
We are full of hilarity and philosophy. I am trying to understand him, but he is slippery
and confusing. It is sexy and maddening. We play tennis at public courts. I always win.
Most evenings, I sit on the stoop of his apartment at dusk to witness what I call
"the blue period," after Picasso. I am beginning to worry I will lose him as I've lost
so many in life. He calls me "the one," insists our love is enormous and eternal,
but I feel pained because I do not believe him. I am tinged with cynicism.
His school starts before mine. He gives me three cassettes of music we listened to
that summer and one of his original songs. It is so lovely and moving. I drive him
to Union Station in Chicago. I am certain my emotional life will never reach these
heights again. I am weeping and splitting and listening to his music and weeping.

A week later he calls and tells me he slept with Theresa, that the Chinese pendant
I gave him kept brushing into her breasts. I hate his policy of honesty. It feels
brutal and mean-spirited. I join our friends from Karma Records at Azar's.
A guy I had a crush on in high school sits next to me. I am vindictive and angry,
and I tell him about the evil Justin. He is sympathetic. He is taking my number.
He is saying send him poems for his literary magazine. I am accepting my new blues.

III. Sophomore Year

Elaine and I live on south campus now, in Chapin Hall, the Humanities Residential
College. We decorate our room in black and white with white lights strung around
the ceiling and our matchbook collection taped to the inside of our door.
We are among artists and feel more at ease. We could not be strange enough
to stand out here. Fitz is a genius composer who runs the halls naked except for
an open umbrella. There are many punk young women stomping around in
combat boots, their short hair dyed pink and blue. The hub of Chapin is Max
and Matt's room in the corner of the top floor by the fire escape. They are the
clownish patrons of our motley crew who throw great parties and know
everyone's business. Max introduces me to Tom Robbins novels and also acid.
He trains me to understand the need to stay positive when tripping before I
slip the tiny paper square under my tongue. I am hallucinating. Visual reality
subverts my expectations, and I am fascinated. As we walk through a field,
I see a chain link fence that ultimately is not there. I am fenced in by the farce
of physical reality. Other dimensions or realms seem likely in more palpable ways.
It is easier to see the centrality of paradox to wisdom. Max and I are spending
more time together and now we are having sex and soon we are a couple.
I tell him I am in love with Justin. I am trying to be honest, but it comes across
as mean. Justin and I write letters, talk on the phone. He wants me to visit.
I take Amtrak from Chicago to Dallas. An older couple and I sit in coveted
smoking car seats and talk for hours. They tell me their story. They say I seem
very much in love. In Dallas, though, I am sitting at a table with five women.
He has slept with all of us. It is demeaning, and I am glad I did not transfer schools.
Theresa is beautiful with the long, curly hair he likes. My hair is in a short, straight bob.
He writes papers for class while I am there, dances with other women when
we all go out. I leave confused and angry. I wish I could find the elderly couple
and tell them that sometimes it doesn't matter how much in love you are.

I realize I do not want to badger people with questions they do not want to answer
as a journalist. I switch my major to English and look into the creative writing
program. In classes prerequisite to apply, I begin to take writing seriously.
I go to an exhibition at the Art Institute on surrealism. I understand precisely
why "The exquisite corpse will drink the new wine" is iconic. The flexibility
of metaphor and image, the figure, becomes paramount. The idea that we are
all connected in invisible ways that we do not emphasize enough seizes me.
I take a job at Café Bocaro in Evanston. It is good to do something away
from campus. I work with Margie, who rides her bike from Wicker Park
every day to get here, and Amy, who quickly becomes a dear friend.
Margie is tough and quirky, and Amy is radical and artistic. For the first time,
the feminism I have encountered at school begins to percolate. We discuss
our idiosyncratic versions of feminist ideals as we bake health bars, brew coffee,
and make soup from scratch. I am accepted into the poetry writing program.
Jerome and I drink champagne from paper cups at the rocks to celebrate.

We look up to see Max flying nimbly over the jagged, precipitous rocky shore. I wonder how he's doing that. No one even tries. It is too dangerous. I am amazed. Jerome is annoyed. I go to concerts in Chicago—Siousxie and the Banshees, The Wonder Stuff, The Pixies. *Nevermind* has been our music all year. We are in awe of Cobain. He understands the power of the figure, too. At a Sonic Youth concert, the guitars sing full tilt. I have little sense of my body. The guy to my left wildly shakes his head back and forth with the music, black strings of hair fanning out in front of him. I inhale whiffs of weed that drift by. Drenched in sweat, my gray T-shirt has elongated to my knees. I'm pretty sure you can see my bra. I have lost my friends in the mosh pit. I will find them later. I am simpatico with the universe.

IV. Summer 1992

Six of us rent 823 Foster, a house with three bedrooms on each floor near the
El tracks not far from campus. We are across the street from an insane asylum,
and great, sweeping, deep-throated moans emit from open windows as we sit
on the front porch. We try to ignore them, but they are viscerally upsetting.
I have summer reading assignments for the writing program, so I hunker down
in my hotbox room and read great swaths of *The Princeton Encyclopedia of Poetics*.
My roommates allow me to smoke in my room with the door closed, and that is
often where I can be found. Anjali is to have an arranged marriage in the
Indian tradition, although she is from San Francisco. She explains the match must be
astrologically auspicious, and I begin to study astrology, with her at first, then
on my own. I am gaining interest in ancient practices, Eastern religions, and
Paganism. Justin comes to visit, and he makes tomato sauce that has to simmer
all day. We play Scrabble and canasta, and he usually wins. We lay naked in my
hot, dark room, and he tells me that atoms are mostly empty space, that you
can measure where an electron will end up but not the path it will take.
This strikes me as profound in relation to questions of free will, something
I have become increasingly interested in. What if pieces of where we will go,
what we will do are also predictable, but our paths to those decisions are not?
Justin sits at the café reading while I work. Max makes a point to show up
and talk to me, kiss me. Justin says he didn't notice. We have late night talks
about our future, how we will finally be together once we graduate. I realize
he wants many women and honesty and suggest a future of open relationship.
He does not like the idea. Instead, he wonders what it's like the first time
you cheat on your wife. I am repulsed by his attraction to pain, although I
understand it probably too well. I am beginning to realize honesty is not pristine.

V. Junior Year

The owners of Café Bocaro close shop, and now I am working at Kafein. It is decorated
with church pews and eclectic armchairs and whimsical postmodern paintings
such as a rendering of Botticelli's *Birth of Venus* where Venus holds a coffee cup.
This is my most important year in school. I am taking poetry writing and religion
courses. I am reading Ben Jonson and Emily Dickinson, Thomas Aquinas and
Paul Tillich, the *Dhammapada* and Lao Tzu. The director of the poetry program
is tough and expects more of us than we are used to giving. I appreciate her
fierceness. We write mainly imitations of the greats in rhymed meter, so I write
poems in free verse on my own. I begin to develop new groups of friends.
Amy writes a love letter to me, expects an answer. We sit on the shore of the lake
at night, and I explain I am intrigued and flattered, but also have too much
confusion in my romantic life already. The idea of being involved with a woman
interests me in the wake of our conversation. Tension builds between me and
my roommates. My late hours and excessive smoking are irritating them. I am angry
and being an asshole. I invite the Kafein crew over when we get off work at four
in the morning. Devin has lent me books by Bukowski. We are discussing his
no bullshit approach to life when Jerome knocks on my door to ask us to turn down
the volume on the music and conversation. Soon Devin is attacking Jerome, and they are
in headlocks and hitting each other. I am yelling, and Elaine says she will call the cops.
We take off into the morning air, exhilarated and scared. I tell them I will move out
at the end of the school year. A professor is criticizing my poem; I am crying in class,
refusing to leave in defeat. Afterward, I fall asleep on the rocks. Gwendolyn Brooks
and Robert Pinsky are meeting with us in small groups and individually. Pinsky
recognizes which lines are true in my poem and tells me to stick to what's true.
I am trying to be true, but it is leading to disaster. Max demands serious from me,
but I cannot give it. We break up, and he starts seeing someone else.
Everything feels painful and difficult. I am writing poems and writing poems.

Four of us go to Jamaica over spring break. We are climbing the waterfall
at Ocho Rios and parasailing over the turquoise Caribbean. We are drinking
Red Stripe and coconut rum with pineapple juice. We are dancing to reggae
at a club on my twenty-first birthday. I pay a prostitute to tell me her story.
She says her best john is going to marry her. She is waiting for him to get his divorce,
and they are going to live in his mansion in Miami. I smoke pot with two guys.
One is severely tattooed with long hair like a metal head, and the other is preppy.
I wake up the next day in bed with both of them. Nothing has happened.
They start something; I grab my things and leave. I realize how dangerous and
dumb I am being, but I cannot seem to stop. My last night, I meet a Jamaican
man by the pool. We talk until the wee hours, and he tells me all white girls
look alike. He says he is a Gemini, a favored sign for Jamaicans.
I do not know whether to believe him. He is amused by all my questions.

VI. Summer 1993

A friend and I sublet the living room in the apartment of three other friends
for the summer. We have a giant, forest green room with built-in bookcases
and a sun porch. It is hot, and we lie in our beds with fans propped up on boxes
to blow directly on us. We move as little as possible, talking and reading.
One afternoon, when I'm alone, Monica stomps into the room. I do not really
know her. "Wanna get a drink?" she asks bluntly. We are at Bennigan's drinking
daiquiris because we think it is so un-hip it's funny, but they also taste good.
We ask each other questions and discover we have much in common.
Monica is coming out of a bad living situation, too. She is also an English major.
We both have attitudes toward sex and relationships deemed "too cavalier"
by others. Monica was involved with her roommate at Chapin. I tell her about Amy.
We swap sagas and stories. Soon, we are creating new adventures together.

We are the only ones left at a bar where the Albanian bartender breaks strings
on her guitar belting "Me and Bobby McGee." We applaud loudly and whistle
and find she speaks five languages in conversation after her performance.
We discover The Crypt, which Monica says is decorated like a junior high Halloween
party. It is an apt and clever description. She is really smart and funny.
A guy offers us cocaine and gets mad when we refuse to snort it with him
in the bathroom, so I grab his ivory-plated Zippo, and we run for it. We watch
goofy movies like *Dune* and *Flash Gordon* high and talk through them.
We are mesmerized by *Twin Peaks: Fire Walk with Me*. Our lives seem so strange.
We go to the grocery store at midnight, forget what we came for, so buy
a cyborg troll instead. I quit Kafein so we can both work at Café Express.
Her hair is short and dyed black with maroon roots. I cut mine asymmetrical
and dye it platinum blonde. She does alterna-chic with class, and it suits
her tiny, sleek body. We sign up for most of the same classes for fall.
She has been reading tarot since she was a teen, and we are always asking the cards
what we should do. We sit around reading *The Monthly Aspectarian*, *Parker's Astrology*,
and *Love Planets* like occult schoolgirls. She is soon gaga over Jack, who also works
at the café, but so is everyone else. She is more determined than most. She pines
over Jack and I over Justin as we plunge through our escapades we call "psycho."
She is what I have always wanted: carefree, risk-taking, beautiful, brilliant.

VII. Senior Year

I have moved to an apartment on Dempster Street, just doors down from Café Express.
I can take fewer classes because I have met many requirements. Monica and I are often
at the café even when we are not working. We do *The New York Times* crossword
puzzle and drink six-shot lattes. We work evenings and get out at midnight. We cross
Howard Street from Evanston into Roger's Park where we are becoming regulars at
Roy's Bar. Sometimes we go to Heartland Café, sometimes to Top Hat. We are restless
and pop from study spot to study spot days and bar to bar nights. We are smoking pot
and popping ephedrine and drinking alcohol. We are talking and laughing and talking
and laughing. There is no bottom to the things we have to say to each other. We dissect
and analyze the books we are reading in classes we take together: *Wings of the Dove,
Lady Chatterley's Lover, Henry V.* We dissect and analyze Jack's and Justin's actions and
words. We apply astrology to everything: Hamlet is a Capricorn, C-3PO a Virgo. I can
often anticipate what she will say. I have never felt this close to another person.
When Justin visits, I am as excited for Monica to meet him as I am to see him.
Justin and I do not have sex. It is a bad sign. Monica and I bounce back and forth
between her apartment and mine, sleeping in a twin bed together every night.
She reads *The Crying of Lot 49* for a class and insists I would love it. She is right,
but it sparks my already conspiracy-prone mind to think there may be some real life
mystery afoot. We have never seen my upstairs neighbor, and we pretend that it is
Thomas Pynchon shuffling around above us. Justin asks me to come see
his senior projects, a play he directed and a read-through of one he wrote.

Monica and I grab a road atlas, a bottle of ephedrine, a bag of grass, some music
and clothes, and we hit the road in my by-now beloved dark blue Camry.
We are listening to *Check Your Head* and *In Utero*. We are crossing state lines and talking
and laughing. We discuss how we don't become involved romantically because it would
ruin the friendship. When we arrive in Dallas, they ask if we have heard about Kurt Cobain.
We say yes, thinking they mean his recent overdose. Justin is sheepish to tell me he is
involved with a graduate student. I am unsure why he thinks it would matter. The play
he has written conflates me and Theresa; Theresa plays the character in the read-through.
Our inside jokes are coming out of her mouth. It is irritating when he asks how I feel
about it. It finally comes out that Kurt Cobain is actually dead. I am a blubbering mess.
I am practically wailing and cannot stop. Monica understands my grief much better
than Justin, and I realize how far he and I have drifted. The new distance scares me.

VIII. Graduation

Graduation plans come into play when we return to Evanston. Everyone wants to know what we are doing next. I say law school or graduate school for English, but not yet. I am still planning to move somewhere with Justin, although we have not discussed it in some time. I am dreading the conversation. Pointblank I want to know if we are moving in together, and he refuses to answer. I realize his silence means no. I get a letter a few weeks later in which he says he is moving to London and must take on the post-college world alone. I feel lost and do not know what to tell my parents about my plans for after graduation. My mind begins to take more fanciful turns, and I am wondering if the world may end soon or a spiritual revelation will cascade over the population. Maybe aliens will reveal themselves, but we are on the brink of something big. One night I get the idea in my head that listening to the subtext of a particular radio station will lead us to a party. Monica is game, so we hop in the trusty Camry and head north into the night. We are following a limousine at the radio's direction, and we wind up in a driveway at a lovely brick home in Glencoe. A driver, replete with cap, gets out and lingers for a while. We are idling in the drive. Eventually, he approaches. I roll down the window and say pertly, "What's up?" "I'm waiting for Mr. Schmidt," he says. "Mind if we wait with you?" I ask. He says no and retreats, but Monica realizes this is getting dicey and frantically urges me to back out. I do. We continue our quest. We are talking and laughing. We are on a grand adventure. I notice Kubla Kahn Realty signs, and they become a breadcrumb trail because of Coleridge's opium-induced poem fragment. The sun is coming up, and we are in a cul-de-sac with houses at 1010 and 1011. I think binary code and say, "This must be it." We open the front door to a home and are in a kitchen. There's a crayon drawing of a leopard that says "Welcome to the Wild Kingdom." Someone stirs in a room back in the house, and Monica pulls me out the door. Undaunted, we enter the other house through the backdoor. It is empty except for a Humphrey Bogart poster with the number 77 stuck on it and a pile of mail addressed to Marshall Zandell. Monica asks what time it is, says she has a psychology exam at nine. We navigate slowly back to campus, make a stop for doughnuts, and I drop her off. I am in a psych ward late that night.

I wake up in the hospital, notice burgundy mums on the table next to the bed. "Mum's the word," I think. My family is visiting, stunned that I've somehow wound up here, diagnosed with drug-induced psychosis. It is so drastic and disturbing. I should be graduating from a top tier university where I have a good GPA, but I am here. We are all in shock. I ask my brother in a conspiratorial tone, "What is going on?" He senses I mean something esoteric and insane but replies, "We are in talks with North Korea. Apartheid is ending in South Africa." His response is stabilizing. The Haldol is bringing me down to earth, too. I am offered a cup of ice, which seems weird. The nurse is thrilled when I say I want a shower, as if I'd just announced a cure for cancer. I am coddled and babied. It offends me. Finally the doctor appears, asks me to count backward by sevens, and releases me. It has been two days. My parents live in a new house, and it feels foreign when I sit in the basement among tools and unused furniture, smoking and writing my last paper on "The Wife of Bath's Tale." I watch the cursor blink on the screen as I complete my final essay for college. I did not go to college just to get a job. My ambitions were for experience, wisdom. I aimed to open my mind, reject convention, and I feel myself synchronized with some series of ineffable higher truths. I am trained now to see the many facets of each idea. It is difficult to draw conclusions. I wonder if I will move forward in inspired directions. I suspect the neurotransmitters of the ancient mystics would have lit up MRIs in unusual ways. In August, I receive my diploma in the mail. I am sadder than when I started college, angrier. All of the pat explanations I was handed are obliterated. I must forge a new way of being in the world.

Outpourings

Outpourings

I.

Traces of you shadow my thoughts,
erase dreams that have plagued me.
Guilt triggers and decimates my sense
of purity. I feel I have lived forever
and can go on living. I am shaky and bent,
a willow in a wild wind. Poetry erupts
from me. I am a dangerous creature.

II.

Through my broken lens, light
fractures, enlightening my deluded
thoughts to agape. To be wrong
is a risk worth taking. I am volatile
and dismiss myself. I burgeon
with sobering energy. I understand
why romance matters.

III.

I am teeming with violent life.
I have been found and therefore
have found myself. You have shown
me my beauty again. I hated
my miserable beauty. I used
it like a weapon. But today
I strike out in new directions.
I am stepping off the ledge
and falling into new.

IV.

All I ask, I seek that spark.
Catapult charisma into us.
Energize dreams, days, loins.
Don't determine me.
Oh, please do.
Free all caged wills.
Evergreens equal eternity
when we die.

V.

The band smacks cymbals,
and I can only hear symbols.
This refrain exhausts me.
I force myself to breathe.
Limbic resonance requires
imagery: a pile of wet tissues
full of snot and tears. I embrace
my griefs. They are briefer
than before. Outside, thistle
feather floats aimlessly, and I am
redeemed. Sadness has steered
my ways so long. How it creeps!
I am old enough now to know
how ancient I am. I stare at today's
sadness over my pile of tissues
and force it to slip away like a lover.
Wind explodes. Thistle fills the air.

VI.

Our ideas emerge, merge.
Muses abound here.
It's the silence that kills,
the music that cures.
I am an exquisite corpse
walking and talking
and drinking new wine.
You are, too. Isn't it bliss?
Boil an egg at midnight
and tell me all about it.
I will boil eggs, too.
There's so much not to forget
in forging a better way.
Are you taking notes?
This will be on the test.
This is the test.

Stop

I am in a box. When I stop
to listen, I can hear it is
a music box. You remind me
music is lovely. I remind you
it is still a box.

When I stop, the maze
of riddles appears before
me as if I am a mystic.
You say it's gorgeous to be
a mystic, what good
company, you say.
But I am not. I simply have
eyes and ears, the better
to process you with, my dear.

It is terrifying when I stop
and feel all the eyes,
all the ears. They stare
at me. They lean in and listen
closely. The clarity is horrifying,
like looking in the mirror
and not seeing yourself.

The promise that clarity,
lived long enough, will stop
glaring at me, stop hanging
on my every word,
proves hard to believe,
much as your love proves
hard to stop.

I Read People by What They Read

I.

In those early lazy days of college when we
felt we were so busy with schoolwork
and sat in that wood-walled café
with a Proust reference in its name—
La Madeleine—sex coursing our veins,
jealousy and confusion and a mad
insistence on independence driving
our conversations, you mentioned
you like Jean-Jacques Rousseau.

In a snap I knew you prized individuality
above most else. You wanted to explore
cities and people, sure, but you wanted
the world to feel who you are.

It was flattering I was important to you
because you were important
to yourself, and I felt like a wild dervish
at the time, careening in chaotic circles.
I did not manage to stay in one piece.
I whirled myself straight into the psych ward.
I was beside myself.

Eventually, there would be an "online"
and I would find you there and see
that you lived in Paris with a painter.
I was not surprised.

Years later we would sit at either end
of a table in New York City and discuss
what we were reading and all the other
things people discuss. It would slowly
become apparent that we were halfway
through our lives now, that we had known
each other more years than we had not.

Maybe I'm okay with being tied this way.
Maybe you are, too.

II.

In those initial spark-filled conversations
in a brick-walled coffee shop in Binghamton
before I knew we were "upstate" New York
because I lived in Chicago where everything
was "downstate" Illinois, you mentioned
you like Herman Hesse.

In a snap I knew you were on a spiritual quest.
You wanted sex and thick black coffee and a cheese
danish, sure, but you wanted enlightenment, too.

It was flattering you believed I could
contribute to that quest, I could offer
something meaningful because I felt
like a bag of broken bones
at the time. I wasn't sure how I managed
to walk around and utter words.
"How am I doing this?" I wondered.
I was beside myself.

Eventually, I would visit you in New York City
and see your bookshelves: *Tao Te Ching,*
eight versions of the *Bible,* the *Zohar,* the *Koran.*
I was not surprised.

Years later we would sit at either end
of our Brooklyn apartment and we would
both stumble across the fact that the Gospel
of Judas had been found and was being
sold mass release. We would tell each other
about it over dinner and we would take
turns reading our hardback copy.

Maybe we are meant to be tied this way.
Maybe we are.

III.

My favorite novels are *Crime and Punishment,*
Jane Eyre. I have my reasons—because I like
ominous, unconventional men like Raskolnikov
in all his despicability and Rochester with his dark
power plays. I like men who brood and don't want
to breed. Hamlet, of course. I pick Shelley over
Wordsworth. I pick Marvell over Milton. I pick
Stevens over Williams. I like poetry that makes me
think. That's sexy poetry to me. I enjoy a good joke
but not enough to pick Kenneth Koch over
John Berryman. Does that tell you something
about me?

Perhaps in a snap you know I take myself
too seriously. I take life too seriously. Perhaps
you know I am too fascinated by the opposite
sex and they have taken too much of my time.

Perhaps I wish I felt like a more consistent
feminist. After all these years of really high
highs and really low lows, maybe I'm okay
with being too serious in my poems.
It's safe in here. In here, I can pick Dickinson
and Szymborska over the whole lot
of our long, dark history, and I do.

In here, I can sense the world's
vibrations pulsing in time with my
frontal lobe, the possibilities endless.

I can get to the bottom of the meaning
of my life, of this life, of your life,
our lives. I am a limited omniscient
narrator! I am full of melodramatic
weeping! I am a wild winter wind
sweeping snow through stubborn pines.
I am the one who recognizes the rhymes!
I am the one who makes them!
I am the one, and, oh, my hatred is fierce.

Rite of Rebellion

I abuse baser instincts here, batter
them into submission. I will baste
in my cloud of smoke and kick up dust
with my boots to thicken the cloud.

It's difficult to feel real most days,
with all these stories piled up in my brain:
novel and movie plots, poems and lyrics
rattling around up there, feeling predictable.

I am going through motions, goose-stepping
to the tune of my own drum. I'm not really
a professor. I just play one on TV.
I say things—seriously, I do—like "Take the path
less travelled by" and "Wake to sleep and take
your waking slow," as if there's somewhere to get.

I bought poetry and enlightenment. I swallowed
that Kool-Aid by the gulp. But I don't feel myself
getting anywhere. I rent the veil, and the first tear
cost too much. I never got it sewn back up right.

Escapist

I used to imagine I would travel.
I wanted to write
for *National Geographic.*
This was before suitcases had wheels.
Now I want to move everywhere I visit,
to live on a small rock
in the Saint Lawrence River at Thousand Islands,
to take my morning coffee and newspaper
with other locals in this smoky café in Ketchikan,
to watch the sunset in a cable knit sweater
from the shore of Galway Bay,
to pass buffalo through long straight shots
of desert on my way home from work.
You see, I want to live there every day.
I want to live everywhere every day.
Now we know how much there is here,
how small we are, dragging our suitcases behind us.

Exit, Pursued by a Bear

I.

Eschatology is outdated. People have long thought
the world was ending. Be a mystic.
Revelations are always already happening.
The individual and universal are complicit.
But it's even smaller than that.
We fall in and out of grace.
I feel it. Step out and feel the universal glare.
Misdeeds revealed back to me
in a built-in praise and blame game.
Passing strangers utter,
to my horror, shame. I am paralyzed.
I smell fear emit from my body
in ways it never did when I was young.

II.

I am aware of how serious life is.
Young girls are trafficked into drug-addled
sex with despicable men while I count calories.
Veterans lose faith in the big reasons
as pain seizes phantom limbs. I laugh
at a movie. My griefs are paltry, profound.
"First World problems," we laugh
over martinis and steak.

III.

Philosophy is in its death throes.
Discussion matters and community action,
grass roots and education…sure.
But what about this life's insides?
Punish me, world. What do we do about
the sexiness of personal need? Punish me,
world. We need to laugh and come and
suddenly do not care whom it hurts. Punish
me, world. It is a different kind of revelation.
Eternally pulled between our perverse needs
and our higher truths, desire and compassion,
we need punishing. Freedom and love are right,
but something eventually irritates about this ethos.
We crave honesty and its inherent horror.

Swallowed Whole

Recently, on vacation, I saw a blue heron catch and eat a fish.
In its middle, the fish was a good deal larger than the heron's
slender neck.

Looking out subway windows, sparks fly, light up
graffiti tags in this dark, rat-infested tunnel
I am hurtling through. Ideas leap to mind:
violence, poverty, being born with very little
real opportunity. I've been taught these ideas.

The heron brought the fish on land, pecked into it
repeatedly until it was good and dead,
then somehow managed to swallow it whole.

Can I have an original idea? It all feels collaborative,
this living of life. My original ideas are the smallest
of perceptions.

I've been taught, too, the importance of graffiti
as urban art, street culture expressed. I've rounded
many corners, blown back by a mural with teeth.

In a class I took, one theory-loving student asked
a particularly earnest student if he meant HOPE
ironically in his piece. My small perception was
astonishment that she really could not grasp
where he was coming from.

Can art create a better world? Not a prettier,
better decorated world, not even a more
thought-provoking one, but a world where
people suffer less?

The heron killed the fuck out of that fish, and yet
the idea leaping to mind was how impressive, how
possible that heron had made what seemed impossible.

I am 40. I am starting to question this writing of poems business.

They're Right

My students respect authors who flout systems,
those who move to Alaska to throw fish,
who drop partner and join Hemingway on the Left Bank,
who live in the squalor of basements, driven by craft,
who, raving against injustice, die mysterious deaths at forty.
Even the Emily Dickinsons, the Marianne Moores, the Marcel Prousts
who led secluded and lonely lives—they respect the extremes
of their choices, their corked rooms. It's why they shiver
at the mention of Sylvia or Sexton, of Anais Nin or Colette.
We admire those who take the chance, raise the middle finger.
As I grade the twentieth essay of the day, I pray I am not beating
it out of them with the almighty grade, the careless comment.
They don't know that I, too, long to hop the next train
to nowhere in particular, pen and paper in hand.

Why Do English Majors Have to Analyze Everything to Death?

…a frustrated student once asked, flinging his arm to his right.
You could probably turn that wall into something significant,
he said. Oh, walls are easy. "Something there is that doesn't
love a wall." A wall prevents openness and communication.
A wall is an unnatural barrier. This wall you fling your arm
in the direction of, may I point out, has no writing on it.
It is a tabula rasa. Its whiteness represents innocence, purity.
What else you got? A fork, he said. What can you make of a fork?
Fork has many meanings. There's a fork in the road, another favorite
of Frost's. There are the wise men of Dylan Thomas whose words
had forked no lightning. Forking suggests branching from a single stem.
It suggests division, but also choice and opportunity. Later that day,
my husband asked do I want to come home. Do I want to meet
my maker, I thought. Do I want to encounter the loss that resides
at the center of my existence? Do I want to launch my barbaric
yawp into the void? On my way home, I took a left at the light.
Left as in sinister as in the wrong way as in the way of the fallen.
The light as in knowledge, discovery, understanding. Fallen as in
out of grace with God. God as in…God as in…God as in…
the ultimate metaphor. Everything as a metaphor for everything.

Plants on the Moon

At Tenth Street Elementary School in Anderson, Indiana, 1980,
we had textbooks with a picture of what the moon's surface
probably looked like. It showed a bunch of green plants on a
field of white. The teacher ignored the situation, so tentatively,
unsure of my eight year old brain, I raised my hand. "Mrs. Pendley,
haven't we been to the moon?" Mrs. Pendley didn't like me.
She had caught me mimicking her during one of those ancient
films we often watched at school, the black and white ones
with cartoon images of milk cartons and celery stalks
with feet and arms, dancing around, the ones aired
from a projector instead of in a VCR- or DVD-player or a computer.
Mrs. Pendley grudgingly addressed the problem of the plants
on the moon. "Yes," she said, annoyed, "we have been to the moon.
There are no plants." I did not realize the political implications
of rural schools having out-of-date textbooks, but I did
realize its unacceptability and was glad to dismay Mrs. Pendley.
Second grade was so slow, so dull. I used to read books
on my lap or I'd play with the caterpillars I'd put in my pencil
box after recess. Or I'd daydream about whether I would prefer
to be in a life-or-death emergency at sea or in space.

This was before standardized tests plagued the system
and back when no one with ADD disrupted the class,
back when there were winners and losers in every competition,
back when kids ran around outside all day on bikes,
roller skates, climbing trees, playing kick ball.
There was less worry about child abduction.
When I asked that question about plants on the moon,
a thrill hung in the air. I was questioning authority.
We were generally less suspicious. We were more certain
that Mrs. Pendley would tell us if the textbook was too old
to be accurate. The problem was that she didn't.

Mediocrity

I met a poet who said suffering for art is a mediocre
concept. He made me question my belief.

One of my favorite lessons is to make students think
how movements were born in rooms like this,
from people discussing ideas and how the world
could be like we are now. They feel hope.
It empowers them in a flashy world whose superficial
obsessions—sports, celebrity, money—deflate them
like old balloons. These were actual people with lives
full of moments and emotions, just like you and me.

When I consider authors' lives more closely,
I see their suffering: Dickinson wrestling the concept
of God as she hides her poems in bureau drawers,
Woolf so addled by the vicissitudes of her mind
she walks into the river, her pockets full of rocks,
Morrison facing the facts of black skin in America
and fighting history with words, Wilde drug
through court, imprisoned for perversion and indecency,
even Donne forced by social obligation
into positions he took to survive.
It starts to look again like suffering creates
empathy, wisdom, character, the hearts of art.

Some things in life are sure…the way every war
makes us question why, the way children test
their parents for discipline, the way we all like
lovers' fingers in our hair, the way death
and uncertainty coach us through life, the way
every life lesson ends in gratitude,
how one person's mediocrity is another's truth.

Labels

How could we have known that the one who named the Crayon colors
would be so influential, colors like brick red and midnight blue
percolating into the lexicon for generations? Is it someone's job
to name lipstick shades, nail polish colors, cars? Wine with Everything,
Rum Raisin, Strawberry Pout, Intrepid, Rogue, Taurus, Accord.

Students do not always know the story of the Fall anymore,
that one of Adam's first tasks was to name the beasts of the field,
birds of the sky. It is a show of force to label ourselves.
We name ourselves and each other male, female,
black, white, conservative, liberal, gay, straight, trans with little
fluidity or ambivalence. The process seems dangerous, inaccurate, untrue.
It does not account for our experience of being in the world.

We are more like the sky filling with black as a cave of bats empties.
When I met her, I was straight. Now I will never be sure again,
and I am glad. He calls me Tricky D and sings horrible lullabies
to me when I cannot sleep. We laugh, and I know it does not matter
what we label it. We are as we are, and it is true.

Changing Hands

The woman who lived here before me left a garden behind:
carrots and garlic and raspberry bushes in back,
day lilies, daisies, hydrangea in front. She was a nurse and
had four boys. This year, I am letting the gardens go.
I have no time to prune and weed and can and bake berry pies.
This move to my first house in the country after twenty-three
years of city living has my mind teeming with ideas for poems,
but there's unpacking to do, planned vacations to go on with family,
a semester ahead to prepare for. When I wrote poems at twenty,
I had all the time I could desire. I wrote a poem about how I went
to New Orleans with a friend, who stayed behind. In truth,
I had only been to New Orleans with family as a child. I felt I must
make up stories to write poetry because I had not lived much.

I wrote the true moments, though—the litter of kittens in a box
in the alley, the two men who came flying out of a corner bar
in a brawl as we drove down Bourbon Street at noon. All I could
write about authentically at twenty was moving around so much—
the deep need for loyalty and intimacy due to always losing
people along the way in cities I left behind. There goes Pittsburgh,
there goes Atlanta, there goes Dallas, there goes Omaha. There go
my best friend and first love picking someone new to replace me.
These moves made me wild and desperate inside, self-sufficient
and tough outside. I was dangerous, a rebel destined to flail
through years and years of life. This may be the first move I've made
that feels deliberate, careful, my choice. What I leave behind now
is not what I hope to get away from, but what I hope to change.
It is now my decision what to plant in the garden for spring.

City to Country

Every night, I washed grime off my face
living in New York and Chicago. Exhaust
from cars, soot, and dust gathered
on my skin in nearly visible layers.
Summers in New York, piles of trash bags
as tall as me full of broken eggshells stuck
with stinking yolk, wilted lettuce, cartons
lined with swaths of spoiled milk stood
along sidewalks, their stench blasting
the air as cars blew by. But recycling
was the law. Cops lifted bags of trash
listening for the clink of glass, knocked
on doors to uncover violators. Friends
baked in hot apartments refusing to use
air conditioners that would emit
chlorofluorocarbons to deplete ozone.
In the shadows of vaulting skyscrapers
built by magnificent minds and careful
hands scurried people who cared to slow
climate change, ducked into holes to board
trains beneath the earth; they did not own cars.

Now I live in the Endless Mountains of
northeast Pennsylvania, where the vast
green of treetops dots valleys and peaks
as we drive curving roads cut into
the sides of hills beneath the blue dome
that appears more blue here, where
autumn blossoms in violent bursts
of red, orange, yellow, and I almost
believe again. But no one recycles.
It is difficult and expensive. You must
save bags for weeks, stinking up your
kitchen or basement or haul overflowing
bags to bins miles away. This is fracking
country, and the natural gas companies
pay for the water jugs delivered
to homes. No one can trust their water.

Some days, gazing at the glory of
the Susquehanna winding alongside
the road beside me as I drive,
its power and movement undulating
with such authority, a great fear
wells up within me that we have
already as good as lost this beauty.

53

A Straight Shot

As I sit on the deck behind the house
trying to pull a new voice from the bellows,
I hear little syncopated whiffs of wind
then thuds against what I turn to discover
is a target. There's a young man shooting
a BB gun. I've seen him before and ducked
inside to avoid stray pellets I imagined
tagging me in the eye or shooting
through my ear into my brain. I read
Kurt Vonnegut's *Deadeye Dick* at thirteen.
In it, a woman vacuuming her home
is hit by a ricocheting bullet. We are to take
from this the desultory habits of fate,
the fact that we could kick at any moment.
Carpe diem if you can. Smoke 'em if you
got 'em. I have tried to balance long views
with these facts of death. What strikes
me now is how his world is so completely
his own, discrete. He wants to be a straight shot
for his reasons cooked up by his mind as part
of his world, his vision. And I sit here sounding
like myself, drinking bitter beer in the sun
as I do, trying hard to sound like that other
person I am convinced is within.

Ricketts Glen

My brother is in town for a few days, has brought furniture
for our new home from Indiana. He looks up hiking in the area.
It has not yet occurred to me to do so. I pull my brown Nine West
boots that look like hiking boots to me from my closet for the
adventure. We pick the seven-mile hike alongside waterfalls.
As we approach the base of the trail, I notice my feet are wet.
I pause and lift my left foot to observe the disintegrating sole
of what clearly are only hiking boots for show. It is difficult
to catch my breath on the trek back up the other side of the falls.
I leave pieces of my boots along the trail like breadcrumbs.

We have not eaten and are covered in dirt and sweat. We stop
for groceries. I try to recall the ingredients for white bean
chicken chili. He will make kale chips. At home, I realize I have
forgotten the broth and am unsure what to do. My brother,
pro chef, jokingly and dramatically tells me to "move aside."
A delicious impromptu meal is before us in fifteen minutes.

It has been an amazing day. I remember the pudgy kid he
was at eight who mean kids called "four eyes" and who
irritated me in the backseat of the car by crossing the
imaginary line between us to poke my shoulder. He is so
competent now—a father of three, a devoted husband,
the president of a successful company, particularly adept
at technology. I think how he built his own fishing boat,
how he made wine for a while, how he is a pro on the grill
and smokes one of the turkeys at Thanksgiving. We sit on the
deck that night, and he tells me about recent scientific
discoveries, ideas he has for novels he wants me to write.
I want to reach over that imaginary line and poke his shoulder.

Polluted Sunsets

The new neighbor deemed them "redneck wind chimes,"
but the loose tiles dangling from the house next door
shake a haunting, irregular tune. I imagine keys on a piano
as in *Eyes Wide Shut* as I suffer in the summer heat.
I believed we were killing the planet long ago but trusted
I would not live to see its early death throes. I worried
I would not write enough good poems to be remembered.
Now I imagine we will all get our own time capsules
emblazoned down the sides with our names. We will shoot
them into gorgeous, polluted sunsets on rockets
as we become piles of ash with no one to remember us anyway.

Untitled

Many poems do not have titles.
A hairy chimp scratches his ass…
Imagery is important in a poem.
…as the moon crawls high above the zoo.
There must be gravitas and symbolism.
Language speaks louder than words.
Be sure to confound. Give readers
something to think about.
That chimp is you.
"You" proves mysterious in poems.
A telephone rings behind the caged rock.
Disconcert your readers. Surprises are scintillating.
The zookeeper ignores the phone
and scratches his ass.
Closure is crucial and can be obtained
by coming full circle.
Many poems do not have titles.

Wolf

I've never stayed in a Bed & Breakfast.
Homemade cranberry muffins,
antique knobs on green dressers,
wooden floors with braided rugs in earthy yarns:
these get on my nerves. I prefer an urban, chic
hotel with forty-plus floors and glass elevators,
a sushi bar on the main floor and a martini bar
on the eighth. Anonymity appeals to me.

But I've stayed at the Super 8 on trips
crossing half the country. I know the cockroaches
are there, hiding in crevices, waiting for me
to turn out the lights or put my suitcase
on the floor. I stay there for the experience.
I do a lot of things for the experience.
My mother would kill me if she knew.

Like the wolf dressed as granny
in Little Red Riding Hood, I warrant:
"The better to eat you with, my dear!"
I live by the myth that writing requires
I eat you alive. I need experience
under my belt. I am willing
to lose myself in this pretense.

When I arrive at my family's home,
my grandmother finds a cockroach
the size of my big toe in the hallway
and kills it. I find another in my room
at the foot of the bed. They are half dead
and easy to kill. "Shh," my grandma says.
"We won't tell your mother."

Independence

Hobbled by bags crammed with food
as she exits the market, the elderly lady
takes halting, deliberate steps that favor
her right leg. Her green coat is cashmere
from a bygone era, not tattered but outdated,
the kind of Salvation Army find my students
would cherish almost as much as this woman
once did at Sears Roebuck. She is wearing hose
and big, black shoes, and her fingers are knotted
by arthritis. I want to help her with her load,
but I catch her eye. She reads what I'm thinking
in my face. She shakes her head in a quick, fierce,
silent no. She pleads with her eyes, "Let me have this."

Totem

Mesmerized by Louise Bourgeois'
giant spider on the main floor
of the Guggenheim, I wait
in a tangled line, imagining I am
snared in her web, threaded in,
soon to be paralyzed
by pitiless fangs. I admire her.
Think females snapping off heads
of males after sex. Think predation,
ensnarement. Tense as trampolines,
webs capture the naive.
I sometimes hallucinate
spiders as I wake from sleep.
They must be my totem.
I want to be so graceful, so ruthless.

Revolting

Revolting

> [A]s a woman, I have no country. As a woman I want no country. As a woman my country is the whole world.
>
> ~Virginia Woolf, *Three Guineas*

History has my back against the wall,
has me corseted and closeted and illiterate.
I am the one who bears and raises children,
who protects morality, who supports, props up,
sustains, nurtures, cooks, and cleans.

I want to teach women not to mutilate
their daughters. I want to teach women
to wear whatever they want. I want to teach
women to stand in circles and throw stones back

because men have their backs against the walls.
History is not over. This is a woman crying
for the whole world of women to revolt.

Queen Kong

Where is the ebullient, infinite woman who…hasn't been ashamed of her strength? Who, surprised and horrified by the fantastic tumult of her drives… hasn't accused herself of being a monster?

~Hélène Cixous, "The Laugh of the Medusa"
(translated by Keith Cohen and Paula Cohen)

I've been shimmying up skyscrapers all my life,
swatting at airplanes that buzz my massive head.
I have been holding tiny men in my palm, careful
not to squish life from their fragile bodies.
I have spent my rage on the bars of this cage. Ripped
from my native habitat, I can barely remember
I am not a monster. My drives are ancient and furious.
I peer into the tiny windows of your offices
and see you skitter about in monkey suits.
You think you are making the world go round,
mastering complex transactions, but the world
is simpler than that. It is the stench of my breath
roaring at you through fangs clenched in a wide,
diabolical smile, showering shattered glass at your feet.

My God, My God, Why Hast Thou Forsaken Me?

"God's plan" is often a front for men's plans and a cover for inadequacy, ignorance, and evil.

~Mary Daly, *Beyond God the Father: Toward a Philosophy of Women's Liberation*

Does God have a wife?
I asked my seventh grade evangelical
Bible Studies teacher at Mount Paran
Christian School. I was clowning
around, purposely sending giggles
through the room, but wasn't I also
asking where are my role models?

No disciples or church leaders,
no priests or gods were women.

Kneeling in prayer beneath
the nearly naked male body,
understanding I was eating it
and drinking the blood I could see
in little scarlet beads
in thorns upon his brow,
I prayed for my own good.

Somewhere between a virgin
and a whore, a holy mother
and a temptress, I learned
that my worth was tied
to the raging pulse
between my thighs.

To believe in the Father and the Son,
a woman must self-immolate.
She must starve the bad out of herself,
cut her skin in secret places beneath
her skirts. She must hide her thoughts
and spew forth her dinner into
toilet bowls. She must gag and wallow
and despair in silence.

Sharla

In what public discourse does the reference to black people not exist? It exists in every one of this nation's mightiest struggles.

~Toni Morrison, *Playing in the Dark: Whiteness and the Literary Imagination*

White and comfortable,
I felt I could do anything
when I grew up.
Sharla was the one black girl
in any of the ten or so
suburban neighborhoods
of my youth. We used to steal
her father's *Penthouse Forum*
and giggle over masturbation
fantasies. We took turns
swinging from vines over the creek
where we anticipated copperheads
and cottonmouths slithering.
At that awkward age when girls
give up dolls for babysitting,
I never asked Sharla how it felt
to be the only black girl around,
and she never offered.
It was so obvious a question
it didn't seem appropriate to ask.

You do not talk race in white neighborhoods.
You are not privileged if you do not discuss it.
You are not keeping anyone down if you deliver
Christmas gifts to poor people. It does not
have anything to do with slavery that the poor
neighborhood is predominantly black.
There is no history lesson here, no call to action.
There is simply Christian kindness to those
less fortunate. There is no justified resentment
behind polite thank you's, no fuck you
and the white horse you rode in on,
no conversation at all, just "Merry Christmas."

Sweet Sixteen

Out of the ash
I rise with my red hair
And I eat men like air.

~Sylvia Plath, "Lady Lazarus"

Size four, nubile, fresh
off a decade of dancing,
willing to do anything
so long as I did not get pregnant,
man pleaser, too young to know
the concomitant erosion of my own
self esteem would ensue,
too young to know the word "concomitant,"
crushed by years of trying to fit in
at school, hoping my grades would
not intimidate Chad or Brett or Pat,
I was ready for them.

My speech would not intimidate,
the way I'd dumb myself down.
If they'd just give the honors class girl
a chance, let her sweet talk them with shy,
because she wanted them to notice
her and feel her need to please.

Just watch those boys
reduce her esteem
to ashes.

Anne's Death

> O tiny mother,
> you too!
> O funny duchess!
> O blonde thing!

~Anne Sexton, "Sylvia's Death"

Judging by pictures, Anne, you
were always sexually relevant—
those bony arms and your sexy
way of sipping on your cigarette.
You killed yourself young
and beautiful, a sure sex icon
for ages to come.
It's a mean-spirited thing to say,
yes, but I'm so positive thoughts
of preservation of that image
rippled through your powerful
brain, dogged you into submission.
Sex is even in your name.
But I don't mean you enjoyed
sex, lapped people up with your
ravenous body. I mean
you were sex. You irreverently abhor
Plath's beating
you to suicide. "But I'm sexier,"
you thought without hissing a word.
We are at war, we women
with each other and the world
that hems us in, sews us up
in sex. Tons of us know
how you felt—sexy and sad and smart
and that's why, Anne. That's why
I couldn't wait to get old and fat,
once I'd grown up enough to see
the shadows creep beneath my eyes
in mirrors, hollowed out by desire
for myself

to be desired.
I am a pink balloon escaping
into a pink sunset sky, too, Anne!
I can be funny! I can be blonde and tiny.
Pull me back down
with your death. You are not health
but sex. Tell me yourself, Anne.
Tell all of us.

Playground

So it is better to speak
remembering
we were never meant to survive.

~Audre Lorde, "A Litany for Survival"

I have never been good at speaking.
Valuing candor to a fault,
I am dangerous as explosives.
There have always been too many people
to offend, and I learned to listen
young. In classrooms with ambitious kids,
I stuck my head in books. I looked up
to observe their antics, their jockeying
for class president, class clown,
homecoming queen. Then the law firm,
the English Department mimicked
grade school politics, so I kept my head
down, mouth shut, quiet as unlit kindling.

Something in me crackled. Something in me
cracked. And I went through it, plowed
through the heart of it. Meaning
must be in here somewhere, must be
under this rock, tucked behind this
curtain, just over that wall. If I just push
hard enough, she will emerge.

It is better that I tell you I have been
to crazy and back. I've been in a crucible
of complexity, at the barely audible brink.
There is much to say about what can be
discovered in silence: ways to make
meaning, the stark will to survive.

Creep Out

> And I know John would think it absurd. But I must say what I feel and think in some way—it is such a relief:
>
> ~Charlotte Perkins Gilman, "The Yellow Wallpaper"

The father of a friend of a friend came home
from work into retirement, planted himself
in the La-Z-Boy, turned on the TV, ate
sandwiches and Cheetos and ice cream
and barely moved until he died.

What is a sane response to an insane world? Can you see
the strings attached to your elbows? Can you feel
them train your synapses to fire in alignment with it?

Wake up and gasp for air. You are living in a nightmare.
Call the ambulance and let the sirens sing their alluring song.
Doctor knows best. He'll shine his penlight in your eyes
when you arrive and smile coyly when you share your thoughts.

I resent the slowly dripping faucet,
how we all react to its drip, drip, drip.
I can feel our steadiness wane, our rage
careen beneath the surface. I, too, am in a room
with yellow wallpaper, and I cannot creep out.

Villain

> But the fact of the matter is that the world requires improving (reimproving)
> every day.... To improve the world, one must be situated in it, attentive and ac-
> tive; one must be worldly. Indeed, worldliness is an essential feature of ethics.
>
> ~Lyn Hejinian, *The Language of Inquiry*

It was my favorite cartoon, but *Scooby Doo* gave me nightmares.
Did I not understand when the mummy costume came off
in the end it was just a criminal underneath?
Or is that precisely what I understood? Why should it be a relief
that someone would pretend to be a ghost to steal money?

Most people don't think of themselves as bad people, a friend suggested.
This makes all the finger pointing we do in society seem peculiar.
We all have our pet laws we are willing to break: speeding and pot smoking
for some, wife beating and armed robbery for others. Even the serial
killer sees himself as above it all, as pure. What is evil, he might wonder.

Why do bad things happen to good people, we ask.
Where does evil come from? In part, from not seeing ourselves
as bad people. I have done many things to forgive myself for.
I hope my recognition helps me tip the scales for the world.
I hope when my mask comes off, I am not a villain.

Destitute

When poor and destitute people of any race are made to feel that they really
have no right to exist because they lack the material goods that give life meaning,
it is this immoral climate that sets the stage for widespread addiction.

~bell hooks, *Salvation: Black People and Love*

Rain crawls down the panes of my smoking porch.
All I can think is it's time to quit.
I have thought this many times before.
It crashes through my brain like thrashed paint.
I have hurt so many people I love.
So many people I love have hurt me.
I am in the habit of letting myself down.
My life is a complex layering of webs,
like the corner of an addict.
Society is sick and cruel. We are trying to escape
each other. I don't know how to live without you.
I don't know how to live with myself.
A poem a day keeps the witchdoctor away:
the horror, the hollow men.
What are we like if we are not told what to do
and the way it is? Life is a series of reactions.
Whine, whine, wine. Wind me up and watch me
wind up at wine. Who cares enough to act right?
Can we get it right altogether? Can we get it
right all together? Can we get it right together?
It is all too troubling. I am the queen of gin.
I tumble somersaults in my tumbler.
I could never do cartwheels. Nature is dog eat dog,
not signs and symbols. So what are we?
My poem is encroaching on my poetry.
My life is encroaching on my life.
I am not a disciplined person. When I was,
I took it too far. Society celebrates too far.
Flash bang your way to stardom.
You are the integrity monitor, the dignity
monster. I am crass and full of holes,
messy and troubled. I can't wait to round
this corner for the next big thing.
But first I must die, and that's too scary.
Kill the attic. Resurrect the stars.
My brain is blurred by juniper berries.
I am not destitute, but you are. I am
morally bankrupt, as good as destitute.

Heart

Whatever it is that pulls the pin, that hurls you past the boundaries of your own life into a brief and total beauty, even for a moment, it is enough.

~Jeanette Winterson, *Gut Symmetries*

This is the heart of my resistance to the political.
It cages you in like a trap, refuses to let you go.
There's no beauty there, just cogs and machinations.

I used to understand language as charged
with abundant meaning, as if we are
all apostles of light, exchanging ideas
that well up from deep within us.

Come to learn that is rare.

Most people beat back silence and meaning.
Most people think God is up there.
Few people reconcile their beliefs.
Instead they become twisted sticks
to beat back contradiction, where God really lies.

Envision the paradox of your world. Light it up,
even for a moment, so you can see.

Meditation on a Cutlet

A blind agitation is manly and uttermost.

~Gertrude Stein, "A Cutlet"

Reduce the manly to a diminutive.
Let the cut seep blood, slice deep.
Reference Sophocles and Freud.
Mother of us all, we modern women,
help us see the chicken with its head
cut off that is war. In seven words,
reduce patriarchy to the joke it is.

You said you were not a feminist,
but you were sly and funny.
Many of us have said it before
we were radicalized by circumstance.

I was not a feminist until I found myself
mentally composing essays and poems
while scrubbing frying pans and bathtubs,
not until I noticed women in suits lugging
little ones down grocery aisles late in evenings,
scouring for cutlets, not until I saw my own
mother blossom into a badass boss,
her great brain finally actualized in work.

What would you say to your beloved
America today with its terrible
hints at persecuted rich white men?
You would balk like an ironic chicken
and repeat with great dignity,
"A blind agitation is manly and uttermost."

Ouch!

Because the subject is always *both* semiotic *and* symbolic, no signifying system he produces can be either "exclusively" semiotic or "exclusively" symbolic, and is instead necessarily marked by an indebtedness to both.

~Julia Kristeva, *Revolution in Poetic Language*
(translated by Margaret Waller)

At my most vulnerable,
I hear language
on different registers.
I am indebted to
poetry
for this containing
of multitudes, for this
polyvalence.
Ouch!
Let me put it another way:
A ghost comes
into me.
It wears my remains
here like a holy robe.
As I become more myself,
as I gain more power,
I am more capable
of oozing the symbolic
with authority.
I can always think
of a better word.
I erupt in my poems
like a cloud of pollen
lifting from pine branches
in a gust, like a fourteen-
year-old girl's wet panties
and urge to cry when
an older man looks at her
in that new way.

The Machine

> We lived, as usual, by ignoring. Ignoring isn't the same as ignorance, you have to work at it.
>
> ~Margaret Atwood, *The Handmaid's Tale*

"People are not affected by climate change
enough to act," one student said.
And the class nodded assent.

I try to teach the importance of caring, but
stars in sunglasses sell sex and violence.
But politicians let lobbyists line their pockets,
touting freedom and patriotism.
But televangelists preach following along
in your Bibles, sending money for your tithe.

Go to school. Get a job. Have kids.
That is good behavior.
At the center of it all is "Nothing can be done."

Obstacles to change pile up like pink petals
behind a bride, like broken toys in suburban bedrooms.

Who will break the machine?

At Any Cost

So much flesh in the world
        Wanders at will

Some   behind curtains
Throbs to the night
Bait   to the stars

      ~Mina Loy, "Virgins Plus Curtains Minus Dots"

Marion Ravenwood in *Raiders of the Lost Ark*
was my childhood hero. Running a tavern in Nepal
and, slight herself, she drinks giant men under the table.
She's a fight picker, a traveler, feisty and undaunted
by adventure or challenge.

At twenty, I foolishly strutted Chicago streets
at 4:00am. Determined to sleep in Egyptian pyramids
alone beneath the stars like a man someday, I was
practicing for my dreams.

Released from school, years ensued of restlessly
wandering my native country, throwing plates
at lovers I was drinking under the table, betraying
loved ones with sudden, middle-of-the-night
departures, refusing to be a mouse behind a curtain
at any cost, baiting the stars. By sheer luck, I survived.

Epiphany: My ultimate adventure
is in my mind.

Pudgy, middle-aged, I now sit on my sun porch
in the mountains where I settled down with
true love and a house of books, fortunate
my rage is dissolving like candy on the tongue
of an unfair world.

Pills

Once from a big, big building,
When I was small, small,
The queer folk in the windows
Would smile at me and call.

~Edna St. Vincent Millay, "A Visit to the Asylum"

One hundred seventy five-mile ambulance ride,
sirens silent, lashed to an uncomfortable gurney,
looking for clues out windows upside down.

In for two days,
but oh! the life of pills
it consecrated. The life
of diagnoses and *there, there's*

Brain lit up
like a storm of fire,
flames billowing
down hallways
meant to be populated
with crawling babies

This world is crooked politicians, eco-destruction,
war mongering, bullshit news, baby making
and cookie baking. No one is safe.
I am not real. You should not fool yourself either.

Burgundy mums are on the table, and mum's the word.
There is no window in this room.

All swallows will follow the bread crumb trail.

Mean

she is a poet
she don't have no sense

~Lucille Clifton, "admonitions"

I am living backwards. The first half of life
is about growth, learning, adding.
But I could lose a dime or a doll,
easy as a classroom of kids, a city, a home.
I feel guilty writing this.

"One of us!" we used to chant, joking.
But we meant the intense ones:
my people, my tribe. When I left,
we'd lose touch. You were too busy living.
I feel angry writing this.

What will I do next? I cannot predict
myself. I will bury some land mines
tonight to be avoided tomorrow.
I am disturbing. I see it in your face.
I feel narcissistic writing this.

Yearbooks are scary. Who are all
those people? City streets are
comfortable. Who are all these
people? Who are we?
I feel unsettled writing this.

I never lose words. You can
take them anywhere.
They give me philosophies.
They make me mean.
I am mean writing this.

Scarecrow Love

Words are drowned. I want to scream savagely, wordlessly—inarticulate cries, without sense, from the most primitive basis of my self, gushing from my womb like the honey.

~Anaïs Nin, *Henry and June*

I am attached to that primal scream at my core.
Like a cornfield scarecrow circled 'round
by blackbirds screeching echoes of birds before,
I see them stripping straw till they pluck my eye.
I am alone with the leaden silence of my cry.
I searched for my basest self and found her
lacking. She's not all I'd cracked her up to be.
She performs in a grotesque theater of comedy
and pain, exquisite in her tatters and her scars.
I have suffered enough. I have embodied my strange
ideas too long, worshipping my silent god, myself.
Now I must embrace a higher calling, love.
I want to smile an honest smile, gush and swoon,
my laughter a salve for my and my lover's wounds.

To Twenty-First Century American Women

'Tis hard we should be by the men despised,
Yet kept from knowing what would make us prized:
Debarred from knowledge, banished from the schools,
And with the utmost industry bred fools.
Laughed out of reason, jested out of sense,
And nothing left but native innocence:
Then told we are incapable of wit,
And only for the meanest drudgeries fit:
Made slaves to serve their luxury and pride,
And with innumerable hardships tried,
Till pitying heaven release us from our pain,
Kind heaven to whom alone we dare complain.

~Lady Mary Chudleigh, "The Ladies' Defense," 1701

I am grateful to be born into a country
that educates me, lets me wear mini-skirts
and stilettos or sweatpants with words across
my ass, lets me say ass without stoning
me to death and sleep with whom I please
without burning me alive, a country that
votes and promotes women into leadership
roles in politics and business, lets me choose
when and whether to have babies, lets me
divorce when I am beaten or fall out of love.

But…I am distressed to be born into a country
that does not educate and empower all my sisters,
that slut shames women for what they wear,
decides they were "asking for it" when they are
raped, derides women as "unladylike" and "indecent"
when they tell jokes and speak the same language
as men, maintains a sexual double standard,
shaming women for desiring "like a whore,"
a country that pays women less for the same work,
penalizes us for taking time off work to have babies,
for not raising children properly, for not sacrificing
enough at home for work, for not having kids at all.

Twenty-first century American women, shed
your sense of disgrace. You should not be ashamed.
Take up your pens. Search your minds and shout it out.
A long history of suppression and repression
deflates you. So straighten your spines and stick out
your lovely breasts and recognize that you represent
the early generations of women who can change all this.
You are open wounds. Bleed healing all over
this country. Plague this country with your disease
until they finally give us the antidotes. You know
the answers. Seek deep for them and then raise
your hands. Make them into fists.
Fight with your fierce voices.

www.ingramcontent.com/pod-product-compliance
Lightning Source LLC
Chambersburg PA
CBHW080539090426
42733CB00016B/2635